LIGHT OF HEAVEN

SAINTS COLORING BOOK

ADALEE HUDE

Our Sunday Visitor
Huntington, Indiana

25 24 23 22 21   3 4 5 6 7 8 9

Our Sunday Visitor Publishing Division
Our Sunday Visitor, Inc.
200 Noll Plaza
Huntington, IN 46750
www.osv.com
1-800-348-2440

ISBN: 978-1-68192-369-7 (Inventory No. T2208)

Cover design: Amanda Falk
Cover art: Adalee Hude
Interior design: Amanda Falk
Interior art: Adalee Hude

PRINTED IN THE UNITED STATES OF AMERICA

OUR LADY

ST. ELIZABETH

ST. JUDE

ST. PETER

ST. MARY MAGDALENE

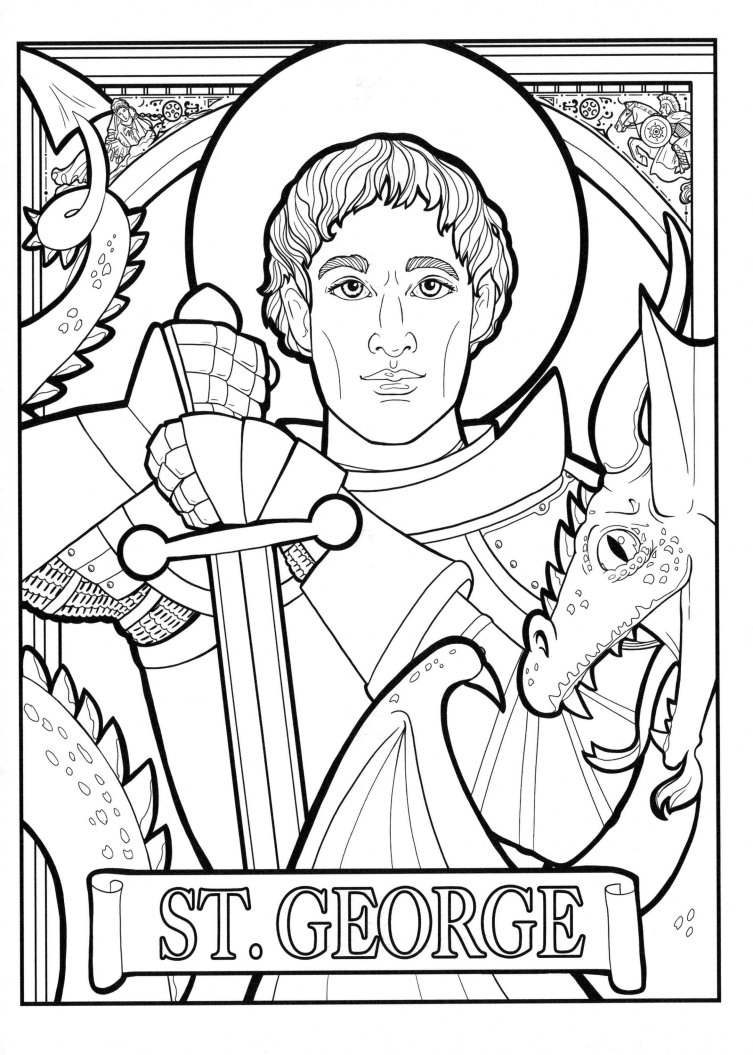

ST. GEORGE

ST. AUGUSTINE

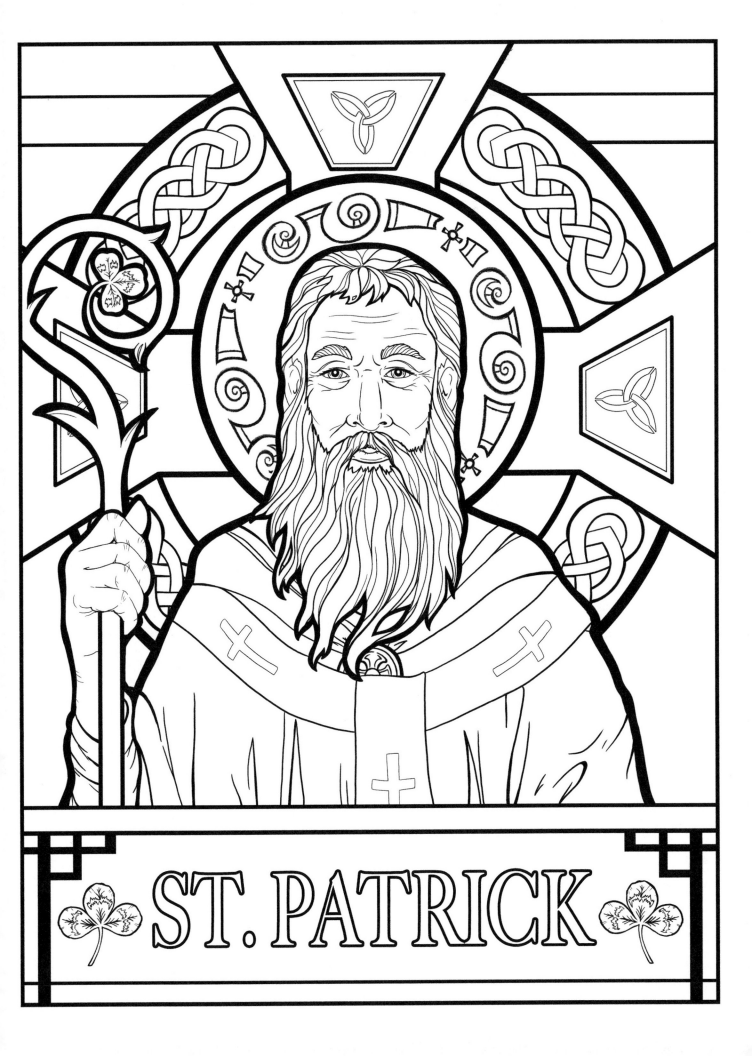

ST. PATRICK

ORA ET LABORA

ST. BENEDICT

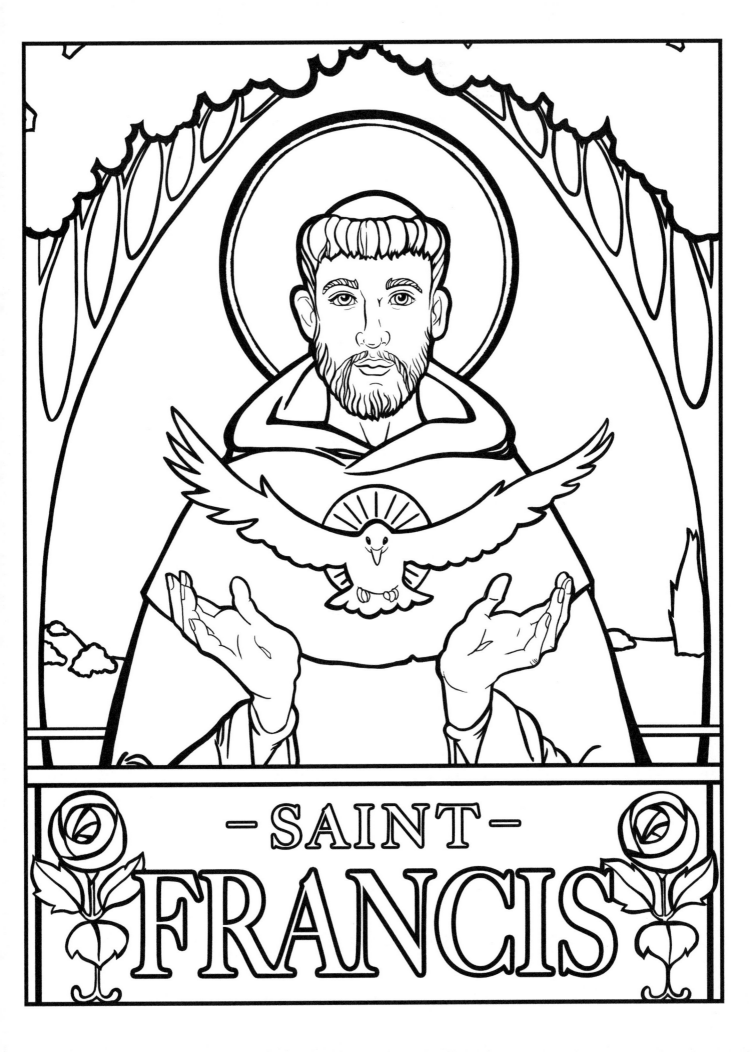

– SAINT –
FRANCIS

- SAINT -
CLARE

ST. CATHERINE

ST. THOMAS
– MORE –

ST. MARTIN

– DE PORRES –

ST. THÉRÈSE

-ST. MARIA-

GORETTI

ST. FAUSTINA

ST. GIANNA

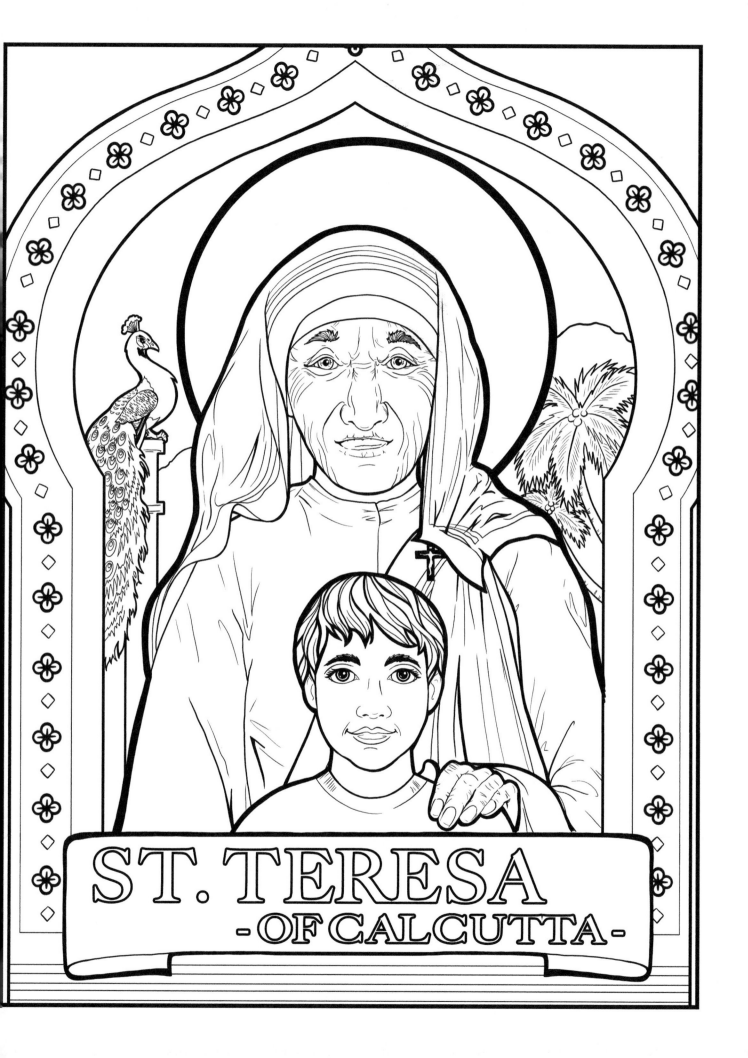

ST. TERESA
-OF CALCUTTA-

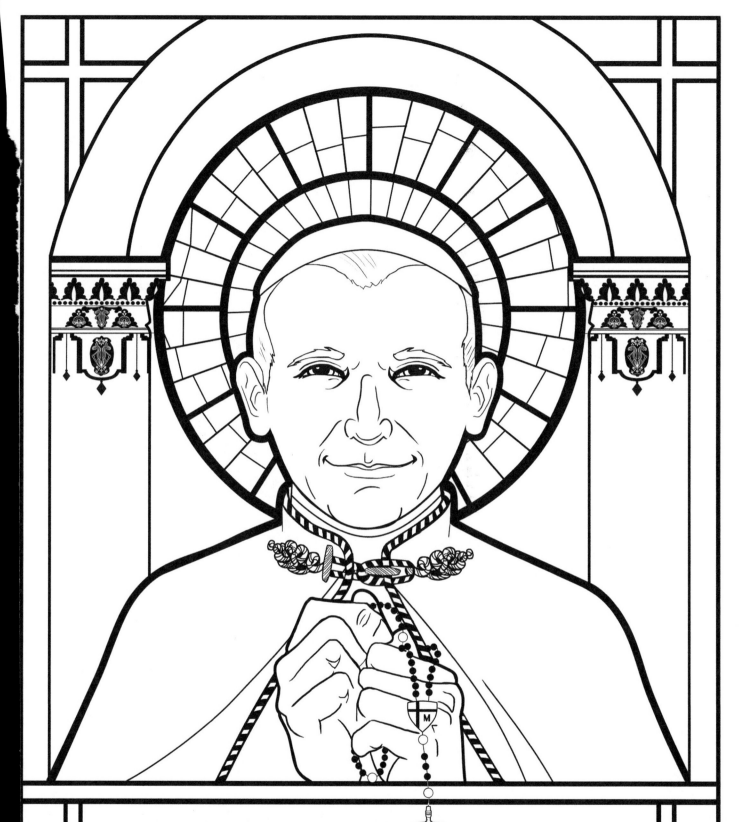

-POPE ST.-
JOHN PAUL II